SOCIAL JUSTICE
AND ACTIVISM

Dr. Mario Joseph

ISBN 979-8-89243-625-0 (paperback)
ISBN 979-8-89243-626-7 (digital)

Christian Faith Publishing
832 Park Avenue
Meadville, PA 16335
www.christianfaithpublishing.com

Printed in the United States of America

CONTENTS

Throughout human history, the quest for justice, equity, equality, and fairness has been a constant endeavor. Societies have risen and fallen, ideologies have clashed, and the yearning for a just world remains undiminished. At the heart of this quest lies the principle of social justice, which seeks to address the imbalances, inequalities, and injustices that pervade our world. For Christians, this principle is not just a societal or political ideal; it is a divine mandate deeply embedded in the teachings and life of Jesus Christ.

Exploring *social justice and activism* is not merely an academic or theoretical exercise. It is a heartfelt journey into the core of Christian beliefs and how they intersect with the pressing issues of our time. How can a believer, inspired by the teachings of Christ, navigate the complex terrains of modern activism? How can the love, compassion, and justice Jesus exemplifies be translated into actionable steps in today's world? These are the questions that this discourse seeks to address.

The world we live in is fraught with challenges. Marginalized communities face systemic oppression, discrimination, and a lack of access to fundamental human rights. In such a scenario, can Christians remain passive observers? As this exploration will reveal, the answer is a resounding *no*. The call to action, to stand in solidarity with the oppressed and to champion the cause of justice, is as relevant today as it was in the times of the early Church.

However, this is a journey with its challenges. Modern activism is multifaceted, often requiring a nuanced understanding of sociopolitical dynamics, cultural contexts, and the intricacies of global issues.

But at its core, the essence remains unchanged: to reflect the love of Christ in every action, every protest, every advocacy effort, and every gesture of support.

This preface invites readers, whether seasoned activists or individuals new to social justice, to explore the Christian perspective on these issues. It is a call to introspection, to reevaluate our understanding of justice, and to be inspired by the transformative power of faith in action. As you journey through these pages, may you be challenged, inspired, and equipped to be a beacon of hope, love, and justice in a world that so desperately needs it. In Micah 6:8, "He has shown you, O mortal, what is good. And what does the Lord require of you? To act justly, love mercy, and walk humbly with your God."

In the face of societal challenges and injustices, the Christian call to social justice and activism is not just a moral imperative but a spiritual vocation. Throughout history, the teachings of Jesus Christ have illuminated the path for countless believers, guiding them in their pursuit of justice, equity, and love for all of God's creation. As we reflect on the myriad ways Christians can engage in social justice movements and support marginalized communities, it becomes evident that the essence of these actions is deeply rooted in the Gospel's core message.

The journey of advocating for justice, while challenging, is a testament to the transformative power of faith in action. By standing in solidarity with the oppressed, speaking out against injustices, and working towards systemic change, Christians are not merely participating in societal movements but living out Christ's command to love one's neighbor as oneself. This love transcends borders, cultures, and socioeconomic backgrounds and serves as a beacon of hope in a world often marred by division and strife.

Furthermore, the integration of faith and activism offers a unique perspective, emphasizing the need for external societal change but also the internal transformation of the heart. It is a reminder that true justice is not just about policies and systems but also about fostering understanding, compassion, and reconciliation among individuals and communities.

The call to social justice and activism for Christians is both a responsibility and a privilege. It is an opportunity to reflect the love of Christ in tangible ways, bridging divides and bringing about healing in a fractured world. As believers continue to navigate the complexities of modern-day activism, may they be continually inspired and guided by Christ's unwavering love and justice, ensuring that their efforts transform societies and draw individuals closer to the heart of God.

ACKNOWLEDGMENTS

I want to glorify God the Father, the Son, and the Holy Spirit for guiding and inspiring me to write this book. I wish to thank my beautiful wife, my best friend, the love of my life for more than thirty years, my five sons, and many family members to whom I am grateful, for supporting me in my service to God since, probably, the moment I became a born-again Christian. The support and encouragement I received in the process are over the top. The patience with the time constraints on family times and schedules is nothing short of an inspiration and a blessing.

The Bethel Haitian Baptist Church of East Orange, where I have served in various leadership positions for more than a decade, and the opportunity to work with young people is a blessing for me and my family. The leaders, brothers, and sisters have regularly lifted me in prayers. In this endeavor, I was inspired to pursue graduate studies. I found the Epic Youth Nations to encourage young Christians to connect their gifts in service, make service a faith practice, and be a blessing to their respective communities.

The gratitude in my heart for the support, love, prayers, and interest shown in my services is paramount. I pray that this book speaks the love, compassion, and justice of Jesus Christ directly to the heart of any believer or anyone who reads it and furthers their understanding of social justice and activism.

INTRODUCTION

In a world of disparities, injustices, and societal challenges, the call for social justice rings louder than ever. From the bustling streets of urban centers to the quiet corners of rural landscapes, the yearning for equality, fairness, and justice is palpable. But where does Christianity, with its rich tapestry of teachings on love, compassion, and righteousness, fit into this mosaic of social activism?

The essence of Christianity is encapsulated in the teachings and life of Jesus Christ—a figure who consistently championed the cause of the marginalized, the oppressed, and the downtrodden throughout His time on earth. His ministry was not confined to the spiritual realm alone; it was deeply intertwined with the social fabric of the times, addressing issues of injustice, inequality, and societal prejudices. In essence, Jesus was not just a spiritual leader; He was a social activist.

This exploration into social justice and activism from a Christian perspective seeks to bridge the millennia-old teachings of the Bible with the contemporary challenges of the twenty-first century. It is an endeavor to understand how believers, armed with the Word of God and a heart full of Christ's love, can navigate the complex terrains of modern-day activism.

The concept of social justice is not foreign to Christian doctrine. The Bible is replete with verses that underscore the importance of justice, mercy, and righteousness. Proverbs 31:8–9 exhorts believers to "speak up for those who cannot speak for themselves, for the rights of all who are destitute. Speak up and judge fairly; defend the rights of the poor and needy." This is not a passive call to acknowl-edge injustice but an active call to address it.

However, in today's world, the landscape of social justice has expanded and evolved. Racial inequality, gender discrimination, environmental justice, and the rights of the LGBTQ+ community, among others, have come to the forefront. For many Christians, this presents both an opportunity and a challenge—an opportunity to extend Christ's love to more communities and to understand and address issues that might not have been prevalent during biblical times.

This discourse is not just a theoretical exploration but a practical guide. It investigates the nuances of modern social justice move-ments, offering insights into how Christians can engage effectively, support marginalized communities, and ensure that their activism truly reflects Christ's love. It is a reminder that Christianity, at its core, is not about passive faith; it's about active love.

As you embark on this journey through the pages of this explo-ration, the hope is that you will be equipped, inspired, challenged, and equipped with the knowledge to address modern societal issues, inspired by the countless believers who have championed the cause of justice throughout history, and questioned to step out of your comfort zone and be an inspiration of hope in a world that so des-perately needs it.

Ultimately, the call to social justice is not just a societal or polit-ical endeavor; it is a divine mandate for Christians. It embodies the commandment to "love your neighbor as yourself" (Mark 12:31) and is a testament to the transformative power of faith in action.

CHAPTER 1

BIBLICAL FOUNDATIONS OF SOCIAL JUSTICE

The concept of social justice, though contemporary in its current expressions, has deep roots in the Christian tradition. The Bible, both in the Old and New Testaments, is full of exhortations and narratives that underscore God's heart for justice, equity, and the upliftment of the marginalized.

"He has shown you, O mortal, what is good. And what does the LORD require of you? To act justly and to love mercy and to walk humbly" (Micah 6:8). This verse from the book of Micah summarizes the essence of social justice from a biblical perspective.

Acting righteously is not merely an external obligation but a reflection of one's relationship with God. It's a call to ensure fairness, equity, and righteousness in interactions with others, especially those sidelined by society. The Old Testament is filled with revolutionary laws and guidelines for their time, emphasizing the protection of the vulnerable. The Israelites were constantly reminded of their history as oppressed people in Egypt and were thus called to treat strangers and foreigners kindly. "Do not oppress a foreigner; you yourselves know how it feels to be foreigners, because you were foreigners in Egypt" (Exodus 23:9). This divine mandate underscores the importance of empathy and compassion in pursuing justice. It's a reminder that the experience of suffering should lead to solidarity, not superiority.

1

The Proverbs, known for their wisdom literature, also touch upon the theme of justice. "Speak up for those who cannot speak for themselves, for the rights of all who are destitute. Speak up and judge fairly; defend the rights of the poor and needy" (Proverbs 31:8–9). Such verses emphasize the proactive nature of justice. It's not enough to refrain from injustice; one must actively advocate for those who are oppressed.

The New Testament continues this theme, with Jesus Christ embodying the principles of justice and love. His ministry was marked by interactions with those disregarded by society: the tax collectors, the sinners, the lepers. Jesus consistently challenged societal norms that perpetuated inequality and oppression. "The Spirit of the Lord is on me, because he has anointed me to proclaim good news to the poor. He has sent me to proclaim freedom for the prisoners and recovery of sight for the blind, to set the oppressed free" (Luke 4:18).

Jesus's proclamation in the synagogue of Nazareth, quoting Isaiah, was an explicit declaration of His mission. It was a mission of justice, liberation, and healing. The Bible provides a robust framework for understanding and engaging in social justice. It transcends time and culture, urging believers to reflect God's heart for justice. As Christians engage in contemporary social justice movements, they are not merely aligning with modern trends. Still, they participate in a divine mandate, echoing the biblical call to "act morally, love mercy, and walk humbly with God."

CHAPTER 2

JESUS: THE ULTIMATE SOCIAL ACTIVIST

The life and teachings of Jesus Christ provide a profound blueprint for Christian engagement in social justice. His ministry, characterized by radical love, compassion, and inclusion, challenges believers to participate in societal transformation actively, ensuring fairness and equity for all. "The Spirit of the Lord is on me, because he has anointed me to proclaim good news to the poor. He has sent me to proclaim freedom for the prisoners and recovery of sight for the blind, to set the oppressed free" (Luke 4:18). This proclamation by Jesus at the beginning of His ministry features His commitment to societal transformation. Jesus positions Himself as an advocate for the marginalized, emphasizing liberation, healing, and justice.

Throughout His ministry, Jesus consistently broke societal norms to uplift the downtrodden. He dined with tax collectors, engaged with Samaritans, and healed on the Sabbath. Each act was a radical statement against the oppressive structures of His time. On hearing this, Jesus said to them, "In your own Law it is written that the testimony of two witnesses is true. I am one who testifies for myself; my other witness is the Father, who sent me" (Mark 2:17–18). In this declaration, Jesus emphasizes His mission to reach the marginalized and ostracized. Jesus challenges the self-righteousness of religious leaders, advocating for an inclusive and compassionate faith.

One of the most poignant examples of Jesus's commitment to social justice is His interaction with the woman caught in adultery. The societal norm would have her stoned, but Jesus challenges the crowd, highlighting their imperfections. "When they kept on questioning him, he straightened up and said to them, 'Let any one of you who is without sin be the first to throw a stone at her'" (John 8:7). This account underlines Jesus's emphasis on mercy over judgment, challenging societal norms perpetuating injustice.

Furthermore, the Parable of the Good Samaritan (Luke 10:25–37) is a powerful lesson on neighborly love that transcends societal divisions. In a society where Samaritans and Jews were at odds, Jesus used a Samaritan to exemplify love and compassion, challenging His listeners to redefine their understanding of "neighbor."

Jesus's teachings on wealth and possessions also touch upon social justice themes. He consistently warned about the dangers of wealth, urging His followers to support the poor and marginalized.

"Sell your possessions and give to the poor. Provide purses for yourselves that will not wear out, a treasure in heaven that will never fail, where no thief comes near and no moth destroys" (Luke 12:33).

The life of Jesus Christ and teachings offer a revolutionary perspective on social justice. He consistently challenged oppressive structures, advocated for the relegated, and emphasized love, compassion, and justice. As modern Christians engage in social justice movements, they are not merely aligning with a contemporary trend but are following in the footsteps of Christ, the ultimate social activist.

CHAPTER 3

HISTORICAL CHRISTIAN ENGAGEMENT IN SOCIAL JUSTICE

T hroughout history, the Christian faith has been a beacon of hope and a catalyst for social change. From the early church's care for the poor to the modern-day fight against global injustices, Christians have been at the forefront of social justice movements, drawing inspiration from the teachings of the Bible. "Religion that God our Father accepts as pure and faultless is this: to look after orphans and widows in their distress and to keep oneself from being polluted by the world" (James 1:27). This verse from the book of James encapsulates the essence of Christian social responsibility. From the earliest days, the church was instructed to care for the most vulnerable in society.

One of the most notable Christian figures in social justice is William Wilberforce. Driven by his deep Christian convictions, Wilberforce led the charge against the transatlantic slave trade in the British Empire. His relentless advocacy, grounded in his faith, eventually led to the abolition of slavery. "Speak up for those who cannot speak for themselves, for the rights of all who are destitute" (Proverbs 31:8).

Inspired by verses like the one cited above, Wilberforce and his contemporaries recognized the biblical mandate to champion the cause of the oppressed. Another pivotal figure in Christian social justice history is Martin Luther King Jr. Drawing from the teach-

5

ings of Jesus and the prophets, King led the civil rights movement in the United States, advocating for the rights and dignity of African Americans. "But let justice roll on like a river, righteousness like a never-failing stream!" (Amos 5:24). King often quoted this verse from Amos, emphasizing the biblical call for justice and equality. His "Letter from Birmingham Jail" is a testament to his deep-rooted Christian beliefs, driving his activism.

In the twentieth century, Mother Teresa stood out as a symbol of Christian compassion and service. Moved by the difficulty of the poor in Calcutta, she dedicated her life to serving the penniless and dying. Her mission, though humanitarian, was deeply spiritual, seeing Christ in the "distressing disguise of the poorest of the poor."

"The King will reply, 'Truly I tell you, whatever you did for one of the least of these brothers and sisters of mine, you did for me'" (Matthew 25:40).

Mother Teresa's work was a living testament to this verse from Matthew. She believed that in serving the poor, she was serving Christ Himself. Numerous grassroots movements and organizations also mark the history of Christian social justice. From establishing hospitals, orphanages, and schools in the early church to modern-day organizations fighting against human trafficking, poverty, and injustice, Christians have consistently risen to the call of social responsibility.

The chronicles of Christian history are crammed with figures and movements that have championed social justice. Drawing inspiration from the Bible, these individuals and groups recognized the intrinsic worth and dignity of every human being, echoing the teachings of Christ. As contemporary Christians navigate the complex landscape of modern social issues, they stand on the shoulders of giants with a rich legacy of faith-driven activism to guide and inspire them.

CHAPTER 4

MODERN CHALLENGES AND THE CHRISTIAN RESPONSE

I n today's rapidly changing world, Christians are confronted with a myriad of social justice challenges. From racial inequality and climate change to refugee crises and human trafficking, the call for justice and righteousness is as pressing as ever. As believers navigate these complex issues, the Bible remains a steadfast guide, illuminating the path of love, compassion, and justice. "Learn to do right; seek justice. Defend the oppressed. Take up the cause of the fatherless; plead the case of the widow" (Isaiah 1:17). This ancient call to justice from the prophet Isaiah resonates profoundly in our contemporary context. It's a clarion call for believers to address societal injustices proactively. Racial inequality remains a pressing issue in many parts of the world.

The recent global movements advocating for racial justice and equality highlight the deep-seated prejudices that persist. As Christians, the Bible's teachings on the inherent worth and dignity of every individual, created in the image of God, should drive our response. "There is neither Jew nor Gentile, neither slave nor free, nor is there male and female, for you are all one in Christ Jesus" (Galatians 3:28). This verse underscores the fundamental Christian belief in the equality of all before God. It challenges believers to actively combat prejudices and work toward a world where everyone is valued and treated justly.

Another pressing challenge is the global refugee crisis. War, persecution, and economic hardships have displaced millions, leading them to seek refuge in foreign lands. The Bible's teachings on hospitality and compassion for the stranger provide a framework for the Christian response. "For I was hungry and you gave me something to eat, I was thirsty and you gave me something to drink, I was a stranger and you invited me in" (Matthew 25:35).

Jesus's words emphasize the importance of extending love and care to those in need, especially the marginalized and displaced. Environmental concerns, particularly climate change, also present significant challenges. As stewards of God's creation, Christians are called to care for the earth and advocate for sustainable practices. "The earth is the LORD's, and everything in it, the world, and all who live in it" (Psalm 24:1). This verse reminds believers of the divine mandate to care for the earth, ensuring its preservation for future generations.

Human trafficking, a grave violation of human rights, is another modern challenge. As advocates of justice and human dignity, Christians are called to combat this evil, echoing the biblical call to "set the oppressed free."

"He upholds the cause of the oppressed and gives food to the hungry. The LORD sets prisoners free" (Psalm 146:7).

While the challenges of the modern world may seem daunting, the Bible provides a robust framework for Christian engagement. It's a call to love, justice, and righteousness, urging believers to be beacons of hope in a world in dire need. As Christians engage in social justice movements, they are not merely responding to contemporary trends but are heeding a timeless, biblical mandate to "act honorably, love mercy, and walk respectfully with God."

CHAPTER 5

THE POWER OF COMPASSIONATE ACTION

In the realm of social justice and activism, compassion is a potent force. It's more than just a feeling; it's a call to action. For Christians, compassionate action is deeply rooted in the teachings and example of Jesus Christ, who consistently reached out to the marginalized, healed the sick, and championed the cause of the oppressed. "When he saw the crowds, he had compassion on them, because they were harassed and helpless, like sheep without a shepherd" (Matthew 9:36).

This verse paints a vivid picture of Jesus's heart. His compassion wasn't passive; it drove Him to teach, heal, and minister to the needs of the people.

Injustices abound in the world of today. The call to compassionate action is more pressing than ever. Whether it's the plight of refugees fleeing conflict, communities grappling with poverty, or individuals facing discrimination, the need for compassionate, Christ-like action is evident. "Carry each other's burdens, and in this way you will fulfill the law of Christ" (Galatians 6:2). This exhortation from Paul underscores the collective responsibility of believers. It's a call to solidarity, to stand with those suffering, and to actively work towards alleviating their burdens.

One of the most potent parables highlighting the essence of compassionate action is the Parable of the Good Samaritan (Luke

10:25–37). In this story, a man is beaten, robbed, and left for dead. While several pass by without helping, the Samaritan, considered an outsider, takes compassionate action. He tends to the man's wounds, provides shelter, and ensures his well-being. "'Which of these three do you think was a neighbor to the man who fell into the hands of robbers?' The expert in the law replied, 'The one who had mercy on him.' Jesus told him, 'Go and do likewise'" (Luke 10:36–37). The message is clear: compassionate action transcends societal boundaries and prejudices. It's a call to "go and do likewise," to be neighbors in the truest sense.

In the modern context, compassionate action can take various forms. It could be supporting initiatives that combat poverty, volunteering in community outreach programs, advocating for policy changes that promote justice, or simply being a voice for the voiceless. "Defend the weak and the fatherless; uphold the cause of the poor and the oppressed. Rescue the weak and the needy; deliver them from the hand of the wicked" (Psalm 82:3–4). These verses from Psalms encapsulate the biblical mandate for compassionate action. It's not just about feeling sympathy; it's about taking steps, big or small, to make a tangible difference.

Compassionate action is at the heart of Christian social justice and activism. It reflects God's love and mercy, channeled through believers to bring about positive change in the world. As Christians engage in various social justice movements, they are not just responding to societal needs but are echoing the compassionate heart of Christ, who said, "The King will reply, 'Truly I tell you, whatever you did for one of the least of these brothers and sisters of mine, you did for me'" (Matthew 25:40)

CHAPTER 6

THE ROLE OF THE CHURCH IN SOCIAL JUSTICE

The church is unequivocally the body of Christ. As such, it has a pivotal role to play in the realm of social justice. Historically, it has been a sanctuary for the oppressed, a voice for the voiceless, and a beacon of hope in tumultuous times. The teachings of the Bible, coupled with the example of Jesus Christ, provide a robust framework for the church's engagement in social justice initiatives. "For just as each of us has one body with many members, and these members do not all have the same function, so in Christ we, though many, form one body, and each member belongs to all the others" (Romans 12:4–5). This verse underscores the collective strength and unity of the church.

Each member, with their unique gifts and talents, contributes to the broader mission of promoting justice, love, and righteousness. The church has been at the forefront of various social justice movements throughout history. From advocating for the abolition of slavery to providing relief during natural disasters, the church has consistently risen to the call of duty, reflecting Christ's love in action. "He has shown you, O mortal, what is good. And what does the LORD require of you? To act justly and to love mercy and to walk humbly with your God" (Micah 6:8). This prophetic call from Micah captures the essence of the church's mission. It's not just about religious rituals or ceremonies but about tangible actions promoting justice, mercy, and humility.

In the modern context, the challenges are multifaceted. Issues like climate change, racial inequality, refugee crises, and economic disparities signal the church to take a stand. And while the challenges are daunting, the church possesses the spiritual and material resources to make a significant impact. "Do not withhold good from those to whom it is due, when it is in your power to act" (Proverbs 3:27). This wisdom from Proverbs is a timely reminder for the church. With its vast network of congregations, resources, and influence, the church is uniquely positioned to champion the cause of the ostracized.

Furthermore, the church serves as a moral compass in society. By grounding its social justice initiatives in the teachings of the Bible, the church offers a perspective that transcends political or societal trends. It's a perspective rooted in eternal truths, emphasizing every individual's intrinsic worth and dignity. "The Spirit of the Sovereign LORD is on me, because the LORD has anointed me to proclaim good news to the poor. He has sent me to bind up the brokenhearted, to proclaim freedom for the captives and release from darkness for the prisoners" (Isaiah 61:1). Echoed by Jesus at the beginning of His ministry, this verse is a clarion call for the church. It's a mandate to bring hope to the hopeless, heal the broken, and give freedom to the oppressed.

The church's role in social justice is not just a peripheral duty; it's central to its mission. As the body of Christ on earth, the church is called to be His hands and feet, reaching out to a world in dire need of justice, love, and hope. As believers engage in various social justice initiatives, they do so not as isolated individuals but as part of a powerful, united body that reflects the very heart of Christ.

CHAPTER 7

PRAYER AND ADVOCACY: TWIN PILLARS OF CHRISTIAN ACTIVISM

I n the journey of social justice and activism, Christians are equipped with two powerful tools: prayer and advocacy (the Blessed Altar). While advocacy propels us into tangible action, prayer anchors our efforts in divine guidance and strength. Together, they form the bedrock of Christian activism, ensuring our endeavors are spiritually grounded and practically impactful. "Then you will call on me and come and pray to me, and I will listen to you" (Jeremiah 29:12).

Prayer is a direct line of communication with God. It's an avenue to seek His wisdom, express our concerns, and intercede on behalf of others. In the context of social justice, prayer becomes even more crucial. Through prayer, believers discern God's heart for the oppressed, gain strength to combat injustices, and find hope in seemingly insurmountable challenges.

On the other hand, advocacy propels believers to be the hands and feet of Jesus in the world. It's about standing up for the rights of the marginalized, raising awareness about pressing issues, and influencing policies for the betterment of society. "Speak up for those who cannot speak for themselves, for the rights of all who are destitute. Speak up and judge fairly; defend the rights of the poor and needy" (Proverbs 31:8–9). This biblical mandate is clear. Advocacy is not an optional endeavor for believers; it's a divine calling. It's about being a voice for the voiceless and ensuring justice prevails.

However, the true power lies in the synergy between prayer and advocacy. Prayer infuses our advocacy efforts with divine insight and power. It reminds us that the ultimate victory belongs to God while we play our part. "In the LORD's hand the king's heart is a stream of water that he channels toward all who please him." (Proverbs 21:1). This verse highlights the sovereignty of God over the affairs of men. While advocacy efforts might target policymakers and leaders, it's through prayer that believers recognize God's ultimate control over their hearts and decisions.

Moreover, prayer cultivates a heart of compassion. As believers spend time in God's presence, they are transformed to see the world through His eyes. This compassion fuels their advocacy efforts, ensuring they are driven by duty and genuine love for the marginalized. "Rejoice always, pray continually, give thanks in all circumstances; for this is God's will for you in Christ Jesus" (1 Thessalonians 5:16–18). This exhortation from Paul captures the essence of the Christian life. It's a life marked by joy, prayer, and gratitude. In social justice, this translates to a relentless pursuit of justice, undergirded by ceaseless prayer and a heart of gratitude for every victory, big or small.

As Christians navigate the complex landscape of social justice and activism, prayer, and advocacy emerge as twin pillars, guiding and strengthening their journey. While advocacy pushes for change in the physical realm, devotion ensures that these efforts are aligned with God's heart and empowered by His might. It's a beautiful dance of faith and action, reflecting the love of Christ in every step.

CHAPTER 8

THE BIBLICAL MANDATE FOR JUSTICE

The call for justice is not a modern phenomenon nor a fleeting trend. It is deeply embedded in the fabric of the Bible, echoing from the Old Testament prophets to the teachings of Jesus in the New Testament. For Christians, pursuing justice is not merely a societal obligation but a divine mandate.

"He has shown you, O mortal, what is good. And what does the LORD require of you? To act justly and to love mercy and to walk humbly?" (Micah 6:8). This verse from the prophet Micah summarizes the spirit of God's expectation for His people.

Justice is not an optional virtue; it's a requirement as essential as love and humility. Throughout the Old Testament, God's heart for the less fortunate is evident. He hears the cries of the oppressed, whether the Israelites in Egyptian bondage or the widows and orphans in society. "Learn to do right; seek justice. Defend the oppressed. Take up the cause of the fatherless; plead the case of the widow" (Isaiah 1:17). Isaiah's words are a clarion call, urging believers to combat oppression and champion the cause of the vulnerable actively. It's a proactive stance, moving beyond mere sympathy to tangible action.

The New Testament further amplifies this call for justice, primarily through the life and teachings of Jesus. Christ consistently aligned Himself with the marginalized, whether dining with tax collectors, healing the sick, or advocating for the oppressed. "Blessed are those who hunger and thirst for righteousness, or they will be filled" (Matthew 5:6). In the Beatitudes, Jesus elevates the pursuit of righteousness and justice. Those who ardently seek it, He promises, will find fulfillment. This is not a passive righteousness but an active, justice-seeking righteousness that challenges societal norms and stands up for the oppressed.

The parable of the Good Samaritan (Luke 10:25–37) further accentuates the Christian mandate for justice. When confronted with the question, "Who is my neighbor?" Jesus responds with a story that shatters cultural boundaries and redefines the concept of neighborly love. It's a call to radical compassion, urging believers to see beyond societal divisions and extend help to all in need. "Religion that God our Father accepts as pure and faultless is this: to look after orphans and widows in their distress and to keep oneself from being polluted by the world" (James 1:27). James, in his epistle, highlights the practical outworking of faith. True religion, he posits, is not just about personal piety but about caring for the marginalized and maintaining moral integrity in a corrupt world.

The biblical mandate for justice is clear and compelling. From Genesis to Revelation, the scriptures resound with God's heart for justice and His call for believers to be its champions. In a world of inequalities and injustices, Christians are divinely commissioned to be bearers of hope, agents of change, and reflections of God's unwavering love for all. As they engage in social justice movements and support marginalized communities, they are not merely fulfilling a societal duty. Still, they are living out a divine mandate, echoing the very heart of God.

CHAPTER 9

EMPATHY AND COMPASSION: THE HEARTBEAT OF CHRISTIAN ACTIVISM

A profound sense of empathy and compassion lies at the core of Christian activism. These virtues, deeply rooted in the teachings and life of Jesus Christ, propel believers to engage in social justice movements and stand in solidarity with marginalized communities. "Rejoice with those who rejoice; mourn with those who mourn" (Romans 12:15). Paul's exhortation to the Romans encapsulates the essence of empathy. It's about feeling with others, sharing their joys and sorrows, and understanding their experiences. This empathetic connection forms the foundation for genuine, impactful activism.

Jesus exemplified this empathy throughout His ministry. Whether He was healing the sick, comforting the grieving, or dining with societal outcasts, Christ consistently showcased a deep compassion for humanity. "When he saw the crowds, he had compassion on them, because they were harassed and helpless, like sheep without a shepherd" (Matthew 9:36). This verse paints a vivid picture of Jesus' heart. The sight of the distressed crowds moved Him deeply, compelling Him to act. This compassion wasn't passive; it translated into healing, teaching, and transformative encounters.

For modern Christians, this Christlike compassion is the driving force behind their social justice endeavors. It's not about jumping on a trendy bandwagon or seeking societal approval. It's about genuinely feeling the pain of the oppressed and being moved to action. The parable of the Good Samaritan (Luke 10:25–37) serves as a poignant reminder of this. The Samaritan, moved by compassion, goes above and beyond to help a wounded stranger. His actions challenge believers to look beyond societal divisions and extend help based on shared humanity. "But a Samaritan, as he traveled, came where the man was; and when he saw him, he took pity on him" (Luke 10:33).

Empathy and compassion also require listening. In the pursuit of justice, Christians must listen to the narratives of the marginalized, understand their struggles, and learn from their experiences.

"My dear brothers and sisters, take note of this: Everyone should be quick to listen, slow to speak and slow to become angry" (James 1:19). James emphasizes the importance of listening, a skill that's indispensable in activism. By listening, believers can better understand the complexities of societal issues and tailor their advocacy efforts accordingly.

Moreover, empathy and compassion extend to those who might oppose or misunderstand social justice initiatives. While it's essential to stand firm in the pursuit of justice, it's equally crucial to approach detractors with love and patience, reflecting Christ's love even in disagreements. "But I tell you, love your enemies and pray for those who persecute you" (Matthew 5:44).

Empathy and compassion are the heartbeat of Christian activism. They ensure that the pursuit of justice is not just about policies and movements but about people. It's about seeing the image of God in every individual, feeling their pain, and being moved to action. As Christians engage in social justice movements, their efforts must continually be fueled by Christlike empathy and compassion, reflecting the profound love of God to a hurting world.

CHAPTER 10

THE POWER OF UNITY: COLLABORATIVE EFFORTS IN CHRISTIAN ACTIVISM

Unity is a formidable force in the vast landscape of social justice and activism. When believers come together, driven by a shared vision and purpose, their collective efforts can bring about transformative change. The Bible, replete with exhortations on unity and collaboration, offers profound insights into the power of collective Christian activism. "How good and pleasant it is when God's people live together in unity!" (Psalm 133:1). This psalm captures the beauty and potency of unity. When believers unite, there's harmony and an amplified impact. Their combined strengths, resources, and passions can tackle societal issues more effectively than isolated efforts.

Jesus Himself prayed for the unity of His followers, understanding their pivotal role in advancing the Kingdom. "My prayer is not for them alone. I pray also for those who will believe in me through their message, that all of them may be one, Father, just as you are in me and I am in you. May they also be in us so that the world may believe that you have sent me" (John 17:20–21). In this prayer, Jesus underscores the evangelistic power of unity. When Christians are united, their collective testimony becomes a compelling witness to the world, drawing many to the love of Christ.

The early church offers a vivid illustration of this. Believers pooled their resources, supported one another, and collectively addressed the needs of their community. "All the believers were together and had everything in common. They sold property and possessions to give to anyone who had need" (Acts 2:44–45). This unity wasn't just about shared resources and a shared mission. They recognized that collaborative efforts were essential to address their society's multifaceted challenges.

In social justice, this unity translates to partnerships between churches, organizations, and individuals. By leveraging each other's strengths, sharing knowledge, and coordinating efforts, they can address systemic issues more holistically. "Two are better than one, because they have a good return for their labor: If either of them falls down, one can help the other up. But pity anyone who falls and has no one to help them up" (Ecclesiastes 4:9–10). Solomon's wisdom highlights the practical benefits of collaboration.

In the challenging journey of activism, having partners offer support, encouragement, and resilience. When one falters, the other can provide strength, ensuring the mission continues unabated. However, unity doesn't imply uniformity. Each believer, Church, or organization brings unique perspectives, skills, and resources. This diversity, when channeled towards a common goal, enriches Christian activism. "As it is, there are many parts, but one body" (1 Corinthians 12:20).

Paul's analogy of the body stresses the value of every member.

In the context of social justice, it's a reminder that every effort, big or small, plays a crucial role in the larger mission. The power of unity in Christian activism is undeniable. As believers collaborate, their combined efforts can bring about lasting change, reflecting the love and justice of Christ in societal issues. In a world marked by divisions, may the church stand as a beacon of unity, showcasing the transformative power of collective Christian activism.

CHAPTER 11

OVERCOMING PERSECUTION: STANDING FIRM IN THE FACE OF OPPOSITION

In the journey of social justice and activism, Christians often encounter opposition. From subtle criticisms to overt persecutions, the path to justice is fraught with challenges. Yet the Bible offers both encouragement and guidance on how believers can navigate these adversities, standing firm in their convictions and reflecting Christ's love amidst opposition. "Blessed are those who are persecuted because of righteousness, for theirs is the kingdom of heaven" (Matthew 5:10). In the Beatitudes, Jesus acknowledges the reality of persecution for those who pursue righteousness.

Yet He also offers a profound promise: a blessing and assurance of the kingdom of heaven. This perspective shifts the narrative from despair to hope, reminding believers of the eternal rewards of their earthly struggles. The early Christians faced intense persecution, from social ostracization to physical harm. Yet their faith remained unshaken, and their commitment to justice and love was unwavering. "Do not be surprised, my brothers and sisters, if the world hates you" (1 John 3:13). John's words to the early Christian community are a sobering reminder that opposition is to be expected.

The world, often at odds with the values of the kingdom, may resist and even resent the transformative work of justice and love.

However, the Bible also offers strategies for navigating this opposition. One of the primary tools is prayer. When faced with threats and persecution, the early Church gathered to pray, seeking God's intervention and strength. "When they heard this, they raised their voices together in prayer to God. 'Sovereign Lord,' they said, 'you made the heavens and the earth and the sea, and everything in them.' Now, Lord, consider their threats and enable your servants to speak your word with great boldness" (Acts 4:24, 29). Their prayer wasn't for the cessation of opposition but for boldness in the face of it. This boldness, rooted in God's power and not human strength, enabled them to continue their mission with renewed vigor.

Another crucial strategy is unity. In the face of external opposition, internal unity becomes a source of strength and encouragement. "May the God who gives endurance and encouragement give you the same attitude of mind toward each other that Christ Jesus had, so that with one mind and one voice you may glorify the God and Father of our Lord Jesus Christ" (Romans 15:5–6). Paul's prayer for the Romans underscores the power of collective resilience. When believers support and uplift each other, they can weather the storms of persecution more effectively.

Lastly, the Bible emphasizes the importance of love, even toward persecutors. This love, radical and countercultural, sets Christian activism apart. "But I tell you, love your enemies and pray for those who persecute you" (Matthew 5:44). Jesus's command to love enemies is a call to reflect His own sacrificial love. In the face of hatred, believers are called to respond with love, transforming enmity into an opportunity for witness.

While persecution and opposition are real challenges in the path of Christian social justice and activism, they are not insurmountable. Armed with prayer, unity, and love and anchored in the promises of Scripture, believers can overcome adversities, advancing the cause of justice, and reflecting the love of Christ in every situation.

CHAPTER 12

BRIDGING THE GAP: ENGAGING WITH SOCIAL JUSTICE ISSUES AS CHRISTIANS

1. Educate and Raise Awareness: Begin by educating the congregation about the biblical basis for social justice. Scriptures such as Micah 6:8, Isaiah 1:17, and Proverbs 31:8–9 emphasize the importance of justice, mercy, and humility.
2. Prayer and Reflection: Dedicate time for collective prayers, seeking guidance and strength to address social injustices. Reflect on the teachings of Jesus, who consistently advocated for the marginalized.
3. Partnerships: Collaborate with local organizations that are already working on social justice issues. This can amplify the impact and reach of your efforts.
4. Host Workshops and Seminars: Organize events that address specific issues like racial inequality, poverty, or environmental justice. Invite experts to provide insights and actionable steps.
5. Support Affected Individuals: Offer counseling, financial assistance, or other resources to those directly affected by social injustices.

Supporting Marginalized Communities:

1. Community Outreach: Organize outreach programs where church members can volunteer in marginalized communities, offering services like tutoring, food distribution, or health clinics.
2. Financial Support: Allocate a portion of the church's budget or organize fundraisers to support initiatives that uplift marginalized communities.
3. Inclusive Ministry: Ensure that church leadership and ministry roles reflect the diversity of the congregation and the broader community.
4. Safe Spaces: Create environments where individuals from marginalized communities can share their experiences and concerns without judgment.
5. Empowerment Programs: Offer programs that provide skills training, mentorship, and resources to help individuals from marginalized communities achieve their goals.

Potential Challenges and Opposition:

1. Misunderstanding of Social Justice: Some may perceive social justice as a political or secular issue rather than a biblical mandate. Addressing this requires education and dialogue. Invite Christian experts in the area to provide insights.
2. Resistance to Change: Long-standing traditions and beliefs can be hard to challenge. It's essential to approach such resistance with patience and understanding.
3. Resource Limitations: While the intent to support may be there, churches might face financial or manpower constraints. Friendly fundraisers are avenues to explore to support in part the mission.
4. External Opposition: There might be external groups or individuals who oppose the church's social justice initia-

tives due to differing beliefs or prejudices. Explore this step with current leaders and stay clear of doctrines.

5. Balancing Act: Ensuring that the pursuit of social justice doesn't overshadow other essential aspects of the church's mission can be challenging. The church's main focus will always be the global preaching of the Gospel of Jesus Christ.

ABOUT THE AUTHOR

D r. Mario Joseph, a devoted Christian author and a community pillar, embodies a life committed to faith, family, and service. Born into the Catholic faith, Mario's spiritual journey would lead him on a remarkable path of devotion and purpose.

In 1993, fate introduced Dr. Mario to Rolaine, who would later become his beloved wife for three decades and the nurturing mother of their five sons. This union was a love story and a catalyst for Dr. Mario's profound transformation. In 1994, under Rolaine's guidance, Dr. Mario made the life-altering decision to accept Jesus Christ as his savior. He symbolized this newfound faith through baptism shortly after that, marking his formal entry into the Bethel Baptist Church as an esteemed member.

Dr. Mario's dedication to his church knew no bounds throughout the years. He wholeheartedly embraced numerous roles, from leading the music department to serving as president of administration and chair of the board of trustees. His versatile talents extended to project management, media production, and sound engineering. Moreover, he inspired and guided the church youth as the coordinator and founder of BHBC Epic Youth Nations.

Dr. Mario's academic achievements are equally impressive, reflecting his commitment to continuous learning. He holds bachelor's degrees in organizational leadership and business administration and master's degrees in organizational leadership and biblical studies. His pursuit of knowledge culminated in a doctor of business administration focused on information technology management. Furthermore, he honed his skills with a mini MBA in digital marketing and certifications in project management, applying for grants, managing, and grants writing.

Beyond his academic and ministry accomplishments, Bethel licenses Dr. Mario to preach the Gospel of Jesus Christ and puts him on the path to pastoral ordination. His life's journey is a testament to unwavering faith, family values, and an unyielding commitment to serving his community and Creator.

Printed in the USA
CPSIA information can be obtained
at www.ICGtesting.com
LVHW091156081124
795950LV00003B/468